I ♥ MUM!

An Odd Squad book for the world's best MUM!

ЯR
RAVETTE PUBLISHING

THE ODD SQUAD and all related characters © 2006
Created by Allan Plenderleith
www.allanplenderleith.com

First Published by
Ravette Publishing Limited 2006
Unit 3, Tristar Centre, Star Road, Partridge Green,
West Sussex RH13 8RA

Printed and bound in Belgium

ISBN 10 : 1-84161-249-9
ISBN 12 : 978-1-84161-249-2

As she approached the cash machine, Mum had the feeling she'd been overspending again.

After a hard day's shopping, the dog makes
the mistake of licking Mum's feet.

Dad treats Mum to a big
bottle of bubbly.

Mum decorates the furniture with that 'distressed' look.

Mum decides to cut down
on the text messaging.

Mum liked to make balloon animals at children's parties - only she didn't use balloons.

In her later years, Lily had to resort to drastic measures to banish wrinkles.

Arriving home late after a night out with the lads,
Dad had the feeling Mum was in a bit of a huff.

Mum finally decides to get a boob job.

Like many women of a certain age, Mum realised her bum had moved south.

Once again, Lily had forgotten to wear her 'boob clips'.

Whilst Mum made cookies for the family,
Fluffy decided to make them 'chocolate chip'.

Whilst walking down the street, Mum accidentally fell into a large crack on the pavement.

To stop her forehead wrinkling, Mum got some buttocks injections.

Caught between two Mums, Billy experiences the phenomenon known as 'Old Lady Wind Vortex'.

Suddenly Mum regretted wearing raspberry lip-gloss on a summer's day.

Mum accidentally displayed her cleavage in public.

THE BONKERS LOGIC OF WOMEN!

CUCKOO!

"ALTHOUGH THIS SKIRT IS PERFECT, I MUST TRY EVERY OTHER STORE BEFORE I COME BACK TO BUY IT!"

Just another 26 shops to try!

"IF I EAT CHIPS OR PUDDING OFF DAD'S PLATE THEY CONTAIN NO CALORIES!"

HEY!

"IF I WRAP THIS JUMPER AROUND MY WAIST NO-ONE WILL NOTICE MY WOBBLY BUTT!"

"IF I SEPARATE MY BUM CHEEKS WHEN I BLOW OFF IT WILL MAKE NO NOISE AND I CAN BLAME THE NEAREST BLOKE!"

At her birthday party, Mum served
some homemade punch.

Mum was just about to say how nice the new hot tub was, when she noticed something.

During the dance, Mum discovered an embarrassing ladder in her tights.

Having slept in again for work, Mum had to apply her make-up on the train.

IF NO-ONE SEES YOU EAT IT,
IT HAS NO CALORIES!

IF YOU HAVE A DIET DRINK WITH A CHOCOLATE BAR, THEY CANCEL EACH OTHER OUT!

IF YOU BREAK A BAR OF CHOCOLATE INTO LITTLE PIECES, THE CALORIES DISAPPEAR!

Things Every Woman should have in her HANDBAG!

AN EMERGENCY GIANT-SIZED CHOCCIE BAR, FOR WHEN THE CRAVINGS COME!

A JAR OF DAD'S BUM GAS TO CLEAR SHOPS OF ANNOYING QUEUES!

DAD'S CREDIT CARD - FOR THOSE ESSENTIAL PURCHASES!

A SMALL POO - FOR SCARING AWAY ANNOYING KIDS!

A BABY MAGAZINE - FOR FRIGHTENING DAD!

To give Dad a treat, Mum dresses up
in her old school uniform.

The irony of life is, the older and weaker Mums get, the stronger their botty burps become.

Mum and her friend always
go to the toilet in pears.

Whilst out with the girls, someone pinched Mum's bum.

Mum wasn't sure whether to be flattered
or insulted about her new earrings from Dad.

Mum had asked the lady in the carpet shop for a sample.

Like most women, Mum was sensitive about the size of her butt.

Mum accidentally sits on one of the annoyingly skinny women at the gym.

Mum finally discovers a
cure for Dad's irritating snoring.

Mum suddenly realised she had something
stuck in her teeth.

To make herself look more buxom, Mum stuffed tissues down her bra.

Men are still turned off by Mum's armpit hair - even when it's arranged in attractive plaits.

To her embarrassment, Mum discovered
she had V.P.L. (Visible Poo Line).

Mum decides to cut down to just one glass of wine a night.

GREAT EXERCISE - As you compare prices in every clothes shop in town!

IMPROVES OBSERVATION - As you hunt for those elusive SALE signs!

STRENGTHENS ARMS

When carrying hundreds of bags loaded with bargains!

IMPROVES SELF-DEFENCE
As you battle the sales vultures for the best bargains!

IMPROVES MATHEMATICAL SKILLS

As you try to work out how much you have left on your credit card

Oops! Mum had actually asked the plastic surgeon to take the *years* off her.

To wind down,
Mum spent all night at the bar.

Mum was adamant that there was no way *her* child had nits.

Clever dog - he had finally found that needle Mum had dropped on the carpet.

Finally, Dad buys Mum something with diamonds.

Mum finally figures out how to put the digital photos on the mantelpiece.

Suddenly, Mum decides to get a face wax.

Mum had a feeling her new high heels were one size too big.

Mum hoped that no-one could tell she was wearing a panty liner.

Thanks to Mum and the family, Dad had no need for expensive satellite navigation.

HOW TO FIGHT THE SIGNS OF AGEING!

Apply wrinkle cream liberally - preferably with a trowel.

Prevent 'Old Lady Tash' by shaving every hour.

Spray regularly with extra strength perfume to mask the smell of decay!

Raise your saggy boobs by tying a couple of knots in them!

MUM – IT'S TIME TO PLAY THE

SPOT YOUR BUM GAME!

THE TINY TUSH:
So thin you can hear the squeal of bone when they sit down.

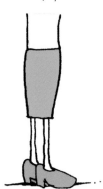

THE LUMPY BUMPY:
As craggy as the moon only no-one wants to explore it.

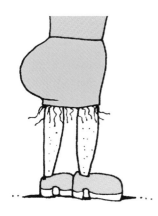

THE HAIRY MARY:
Like the werewolf of the woman world. Must be shaved hourly.

THE SAGGY BAGGY:
Makes an elephant look pert. Can be used to hold cigarettes, pencils and chocolate!

IN A **Mum's** DREAM WORLD...

Dad would only ever buy you shoes or chocolate.

Hairdressers would listen to you.

Chocolate cake would be a diet food!

Their botty blow-offs would smell of roses
and be completely silent.

Other ODD SQUAD books available ...

		ISBN	Price
The Odd Squad's Big Poo Handbook	(hardcover)	1 84161 168 9	£7.99
The Odd Squad's Sexy Sex Manual	(hardcover)	1 84161 220 0	£7.99
The Odd Squad Butt Naked		1 84161 190 5	£3.99
The Odd Squad Gross Out!		1 84161 219 7	£3.99
The Odd Squad's Saggy Bits		1 84161 218 9	£3.99
The REAL Kama Sutra		1 84161 103 4	£3.99
The Odd Squad Volume One		1 85304 936 0	£3.99
I Love Xmas!	(hardcover)	1 84161 262 6	£4.99
I Love Dad!	(hardcover)	1 84161 252 9	£4.99
I Love Poo!	(hardcover)	1 84161 240 5	£4.99
I Love Sex!	(hardcover)	1 84161 241 3	£4.99
I Love Wine!	(hardcover)	1 84161 239 1	£4.99
I Love Beer!	(hardcover)	1 84161 238 3	£4.99
The Odd Squad's Little Book of Booze		1 84161 138 7	£2.50
The Odd Squad's Little Book of Men		1 84161 093 3	£2.50
The Odd Squad's Little Book of Oldies		1 84161 139 5	£2.50
The Odd Squad's Little Book of Poo		1 84161 096 8	£2.50
The Odd Squad's Little Book of Pumping		1 84161 140 9	£2.50
The Odd Squad's Little Book of Sex		1 84161 095 X	£2.50
The Odd Squad's Little Book of Women		1 84161 094 1	£2.50
The Odd Squad's Little Book of X-Rated Cartoons		1 84161 141 7	£2.50

HOW TO ORDER: Please send a cheque/postal order in £ sterling, made payable to 'Ravette Publishing' for the cover price of the books and allow the following for post & packing ...

UK & BFPO	70p for the first book & 40p per book thereafter
Europe & Eire	£1.30 for the first book & 70p per book thereafter
Rest of the world	£2.20 for the first book & £1.10 per book thereafter

RAVETTE PUBLISHING
Unit 3, Tristar Centre, Star Road, Partridge Green, West Sussex RH13 8RA

Prices and availability are subject to change without prior notice.